Qi and Grace

An Embodied Lord's Prayer

by Elise Dirlam Ching & Kaleo Ching
with Reverend Steve Harms

Cover art and illustrations by Kaleo Ching

Photos and design by Elise Dirlam Ching

Practice along with the "Abba-Imma Chi Kung" video at:

www.kaleoching.com/videos.html

www.peacejourney.org/adult-education-forums/

Any Qigong information from Chi and Creativity: Vital Energy and Your Inner Artist, *published by Blue Snake Books, copyright © 2007, and from* The Creative Art of Living, Dying & Renewal: Your Journey Through Stories, Qigong Meditation, Journaling, and Art, *published by North Atlantic Books, copyright © 2014, both by Elise Dirlam Ching and Kaleo Ching, is reprinted by permission of publisher.*

ISBN-13: 978-1515149200
ISBN-10: 151514920X

Mahalo Ke Akua
In Gratitude to the Divine

CONTENTS

MAHALO

To the spirits of our parents and ancestors, who accompany us on life's journey toward deeper connection with the Divine.

To all at Peace Lutheran Church and at San Damiano Retreat Center, both in Danville, California, for the sharing of Qigong for an embodied Lord's prayer.

To Pastor Brenda Bos for creating the Abba-Imma Qigong (Chi Kung) video (2012).

To all the expert and caring staff at North Atlantic books who guided and supported Elise and Kaleo in birthing their books on Qigong and creativity.

PREFACE

Blessings to you on your journey. As you engage *Qi and grace: Qigong for an Embodied Lord's Prayer,* we invite you to do so in a spirit of centeredness and openness – centered in your spiritual practice and your own personal relationship to prayer, yet open to new possibilities as we explore the linguistic and historical context of the words and phrases of the Lord's Prayer and the ancient principles and practices of Qigong.

For the practices and meditations in this manual, go to a pleasing and quiet place where you will not be disturbed. Find a comfortable seated or standing position. Bring your journal and writing tools (and drawing tools if you desire) with you. Record your experience, and note how it changes over time.

When you are ready, we encourage you to share this embodied Lord's Prayer – its sacred words and Qigong movements – with others. Share it with your friends, groups, congregations.

To deepen your experience, Qigong (Chi Kung) foundations may be explored in either of Elise and Kaleo's books, *The Creative Art of Living, Dying, and Renewal: Your Journey through Stories, Qigong Meditation, Journaling, and Art* (© 2014, North Atlantic Books) or *Chi and Creativity: Vital Energy and Your Inner Artist* (© 2007, Blue Snake Books).

The Creative Art of Living, Dying, and Renewal contains stories of people's experiences of Qigong and other healing modalities in life's path through loss and renewal. It includes both fictional and actual examples of healing through hypnotherapy, regression, Qigong, journaling, and expressive art. The Qigong instructions are directed to inspire the reader and offer healing tools for the daily journey of living, dying, and renewal.

Chi and Creativity includes many detailed Qigong foundations and practices, as well as guided visualizations, art, and creativity processes for healing and self-discovery.

Both books include meridians, acupressure points (acupoints), and specific Qigong and meditation techniques to enhance one's life's journey.

Note that, following the guidance of our publisher, between these two books we have converted from the older Wade-Gilles system of romanization of Chinese words to the newer and increasingly familiar Pinyin system. Please pardon the discrepancies in spelling. It is quite Daoist to flow in harmony with changing times.

INTRODUCTION

Why combine the Lord's Prayer and Qigong? After all, this prayer is a religious practice grounded in Jesus' Jewish roots and Christianity's beginnings, while Qigong is a holistic practice which invites spiritual awareness beyond any religious boundaries. Yet embodied prayer is even more ancient than Judaism of Jesus' religious practice and heritage or Qigong with its roots in the *Yijing (I Ching)* – both over three thousand years old.

The practice of integrating prayer and movement extends trans-millennially, trans-culturally, and it transcends religious affiliations. Zen walking meditation is a form of embodied prayer. Hatha Yoga as a branch of the eight-limbed spiritual path of Astanga Yoga is embodied prayer. Sufi whirling is embodied prayer. Hula Kahiko (prior to Western influence), rooted in spiritual tradition and often danced to honor Hawaiian gods or goddesses, is embodied prayer. Such Native American dances as the Sun Dance and the Ghost Dance are embodied prayer.

Our bodies are prayer vessels. At Peace Lutheran Church, Reverend Steve invites us, Kaleo and Elise, to lead the congregation in the Abba-Imma Qigong, the embodied Lord's Prayer, to prepare body and soul for receiving the Eucharist. In Qigong our bodies are conduits between Heaven and Earth.

Christianity acknowledges the Holy Trinity of Father, Son, and Holy Spirit. Qigong has its own triads: the Three Powers of Heaven, Earth, and Human person; the Three Luminaries of

Sun, Moon, and Stars; the Three Dan Tians of body, heart, and mind; the Three Treasures of essence (Jing), vital energy (Qi), and spirit (Shen); the Three Virtues of compassion, moderation, and humility.

Speaking in chorus with the two-thousand-year-old utterance of the Lord's Prayer and moving in harmony with the ancient practice of Qigong, the Abba-Imma Qigong blends Judeo-Christian and Daoist wisdom and compassion for self and others. It enhances your intimacy with the Divine beyond and within.

This practice is grounded in the Daoist and Traditional Chinese Medicine principles of Yin and Yang, the three Dan Tians of body, heart, and mind, and the organ-meridian system of energy with its acu-points near the body's surface.

Abba-Imma Qigong invokes and honors Abba-Imma, the Father-Mother God, the Divine Source, the Universal Spirit. Activating meridians and important acu-points, it draws in the gifts from the Universal Source, the Qi of Heaven, Earth, and Environment. It harmonizes the emotions and summons the triadic synergy of body, psyche, and spirit. It is founded on the teachings of the past, it engages the witnessing awareness of the now, and it sparks the creative potential reaching toward what is yet to come.

Journaling: You and Prayer

What is your relationship to the Lord's Prayer? How has the prayer changed for you over time?

What experience have you had of embodied prayer? Have you engaged in a physical activity that felt also spiritual for you, like dancing, hiking, kayaking, or swimming? Have you engaged in a moving meditation practice like Hatha Yoga or Tai-ji? What shifts have you noticed from your experiences?

STEVE'S JOURNEY AND THE REVISED LORD'S PRAYER

ELISE: What experiences and influences have helped to shape your practice as a spiritual seeker and a Christian minister?

STEVE: A strong influence was my family. I come from four generations of Lutheran clergy. What I appreciate is that the religious influence was never heavy-handed.

I got a very fine theological education, thoroughly immersed in liberal arts and looking at the holistic view of how does this theological heritage integrate into the rest of the world? While at seminary I got involved in theater. The provocative question of theater is "how do you do it and what does it do in your body?" Theological study doesn't engage this.

In 1973 I spent three months on the Rosebud Sioux Reservation between my junior and senior years in college. It was intense and glorious. Words within the Lakota tribe are literally considered pieces of truth. You don't speak unless you're really motivated because you don't want to treat truth carelessly.

In 1980 my wife, Bev, and I spent six months in Asia. That prompted me, in 1985, to return to India to spend a month at Bede Griffith's ashram. I wondered, how was the Christian faith going to be expressed in the context of Hindu roots? Being there was an affirmation of wholeness. It was a community filled with Jains, Buddhists, Hindus, and Christians. The Eucharist was wide open, which was very liberating.

I also spent time at one of Gandhi's ashrams, where the wholeness of his practice had infused the community. The Sermon on the Mount had inspired Gandhi's commitment to nonviolence. It helped him to define what nonviolence meant and to embody the meaning of the Sermon on the Mount himself. He was a living example of complete embodiment – the willingness to bear the suffering of others to liberate all of us. That's what we all need – an experience of grace, wisdom, and love embodied.

In 2001 I went to Ladakh, Western Tibet. What struck me was the humanness of the practice. One of the teachings is that people don't learn wisdom on an empty stomach, so feed people before the wise one speaks. There was a playful interaction between monks and lay people. It was real, it was fun, it was human.

Another teacher, Sifu Choy Kam Man, third generation lineage Taiji master, had a profound influence on me. I studied eight years with him, year round, in San Francisco Chinatown. I came to love Taiji quite quickly for its harmonization of body, breath, mind, and spirit. It nurtures presence in life and in liturgy.

From 1978 to 1988 I worked for the Tenderloin Night Ministry. It was raw – exposure to the worst of life – being present to the impoverished, to what they were suffering and how they are blamed. The worst thing about poverty is that your decisions have no impact on your own life.

The Night Minister came on at 10:00 p.m. to help meet housing needs, address food issues, connect people and resources. From midnight until 2:00 a.m., when the theater people had gone home and the street people took over, that was the liveliest time. There'd be weird things like getting shot at or responding to calls from suicide prevention or police; times of encountering guns to our heads, knives to our faces; getting folks like battered women and other people in crisis to clinics or hospitals; sometimes going to bridges to talk to people considering jumping.

Then I was in theater ministry from 1982 to 1985, touring the country with a drama ministry I initiated called "Rauch," meaning "wind/spirit/breath" in Hebrew. We mostly appeared at conferences to help folks embody a spiritual theme.

ELISE: What and how do all those experiences come together in the Abba-Imma Lord's Prayer?

STEVE: Jesus has been so boxed in by the church, making us assume we know what he was about. For me the gospel dynamic is the incarnational affirmation of people, which is endless. It is said that only love changes people; nothing else does. Unless the heart is touched, the being is not changed. This deep loving was the commitment of Jesus.

There are three hungers in human beings. One is the hunger to experience what is real – truth in a new way. Two is the insatiable hunger for meaning and for experiencing fullness in life – and we need to remember it's insatiable. Three is literal hunger; we are creatures, we live day by day, and that puts me in relationship to others. I think the Lord's Prayer is addressing those three hungers. The God-drive connection is the insatiable hunger and the inspiration. Christ is the embodiment of this infinite compassion – the Divine not afraid to get involved.

The first half of the Lord's Prayer is orienting us. The Second part is the daily bread. The bread is our physical survival but also affirming that being a physical human being is a sacrament. Period. Embodiment means predisposing ourselves to being in the presence of awe.

ELISE: What inspired you to reexamine the wording of the Lord's Prayer?

STEVE: Two things. One, Hebrew and Aramaic are multilayered languages, so each word is carrying multiple meanings. Two, I wanted to communicate a sense of inspiration and connection, which is what this prayer generates.

The Lord's Prayer has too often become a formula and therefore numbing. It conveys a sense of a heavy-handed Jesus, who is offensive for the wrong reasons – an emblem of "repent or go to hell!" Actually he was an embodiment of infinite compassion. This open blessing of all kinds of people is what disturbs folks. It was his wisdom and profound affirmation and mercy toward the Other that made Jesus an outsider, a social critic, and one who had to be eliminated.

So that was the prompt for me: engaging the fullness and the wholeness – to offend or heal people for loving reasons.

ELISE: How did you approach researching the words and authenticating their original meanings?

STEVE: Joachim Jeremias, twentieth century theologian and scholar, did some groundbreaking work with the Lord's Prayer, which was helpful within the Christian theological culture. One of the things he opened up was the notion of "Abba" as an expression of radical intimacy with God. What Jesus is making clear is that God is not "the judge" out to get you, nor the abyss of the philosophers, nor the distant, floating, unattainable nirvana. God is overflowing love. This intimate connection is what changes people – not through an act of appeasement or a step toward perfection, but in deep acceptance of messy grace.

One could say Jesus was the culmination of evolution: the cosmogenic, which led to biogenic, to anthropogenic, finally birthed the Christ, who is embodying Abba, the Source. There is a wholeness with the whole universe that the Lord's Prayer is meant to convey.

REVEREND STEVE: WORDING OF THE ABBA-IMMA LORD'S PRAYER

Abba, Imma, in heaven: To address God in personal terms is a radical innovation by Jesus. The Holy/Numinous is commonly understood as the Majestic and Awe-Inspiring yet distant One. By bringing God close with a familiar name, Jesus acknowledges that Divinity walks among us. The intimacy of "Abba-Imma" is striking, disturbing, and profound. It affirms that we come from God and belong to God. By identifying God as "Abba/Papa" or "Imma/Mama," Jesus encourages us to trust the compassionate God who embraces our concerns with understanding, care, and healing. Imma as the feminine form communicates God's going beyond our gender categories. God has neither masculine image nor patriarchal bias. To cling to an image of God that is exclusive imposes human limitations upon God. Acknowledging that masculine and feminine energies, potentials, and capacities deserve equal attention in any conception we might sustain about God keeps us from diminishing God by half in our awareness.

Holy be your Name: In Judaism the name of God is cannot be spoken because no name can express or capture the Divine. Without names or use of images, Jesus and Judaism seek to honor the Presence and maintain the Mystery by encouraging us to attune ourselves through prayer and stillness as we listen and become aware of who and how the Holy One is among us. "Holy be your Name" also conveys: Let your Name permeate the whole of Reality since You are Reality.

Your reign come: "Basileia" in Greek means "reign" but was translated into English as "kingdom." The latter denotes place, and we got stuck thinking that heaven is some other place rather than a relationship designed to nurture life.

Your yearning be done on earth as it is in heaven: The translation of "will" in English is far too narrow and restrictive. Will implies compliance, obedience, and moral perfection. But "yearning," which is true to the Aramaic, conveys God's longing, ache, and compassionate desire for the best for us. This was the message especially of the Hebrew Prophets – that God is not remote and indifferent to our plight, but God is in anguish over our suffering (personal, existential, relational, and resulting from injustice).

Give us this day the bread we need: At the heart of the prayer is the awareness that we are creatures who live in need of food, shelter, emotional stability, and community. Daily realities are not dismissed as insignificant. "Daily bread" can imply a kind of passivity, as in being handed rations. "The bread we need" is truer to the spirit of the plea. We acknowledge our creature needs and our reliance on the Divine to work through nature and human endeavors toward our fulfillment.

Forgive us our debts as we forgive our debtors: This is the original translation/intent. In Jesus' day the prisons were filled with debtors – the poor – and this is a prayer for release and justice. It, too, is a petition that goes "against the grain" by standing up for the impoverished. Later, "forgive us our sins" became an expanded understanding of the many ways and dimensions in which we hurt and negate each other. If the word "sins" or "debtors" doesn't fit with the spirit of your prayer, the word "wrongs" may be substituted.

Guide us through life's trials: This is the best translation because nobody escapes the Trial of Life. It is asking for the
strength, courage, and steadfastness to continue without being
broken by life. It is a prayer which prays for resistance to res-
ignation and cynicism.

Shelter us all from evil: Evil does not have a separate exis-
tence; it works by corrupting our best efforts. There are dimensions of life which are hidden and elusive and that cannot be
identified but which corrode us with horrific effect. Paul
speaks of this as the "powers and principalities of this world";
Thomas Merton calls it the "Unspeakable." This petition asks
for protection from negating/destructive/scapegoating powers
which we do not see, recognize, or comprehend.

***For the kinship, the power, and the glory are yours, now and
forever:*** "Grace, wisdom, and love" also communicates the
true intent here. Again "kingdom," as opposed to kinship or
grace, misses the point. The gift of Grace or the New Creation
through Christ generates community/kinship and vital energy.
It reveals the Glory of God through the dignity and joy of
Compassionate Community (or the fulfillment of the Jewish
Covenant for Shalom). This was God's desire for us from before the beginning of Creation, it is the blessing of the cruci-
fied and resurrecting Christ, and it is the work and pleasure of
the free-moving Holy Spirit.

Journaling: You and the Abba-Imma Lord's Prayer

As you link these phrases together in this revitalized translation of the Lord's Prayer, how does your mind respond? How does your heart feel? As you reflect on the explanations for the rephrasing, how does your attitude toward this ancient prayer shift?

CONVERSATION WITH KALEO AND ELISE: QIGONG AS EMBODIED PRAYER

ELISE: How did you first experience Taiji and Qigong?

KALEO: My mother was born and raised on a sugar cane plantation on the Big Island of Hawai'i in Kā'ū, near Kīlauea volcano. She loved singing and playing Hawaiian music on her 'ukulele. I inherited her passion for the music and the spirit of the islands. When I was twenty-six years old, studying art at the University of Hawai'i, I watched people doing Taiji on the grass. They moved so gracefully, like in hula, with the rhythms of the earth and soft island breezes. I'd been an avid surfer, and Taiji was like being one with the wave, with the ocean of Qi. Taiji was a way for me to dance my love of Hawai'i and honor my Asian ancestors. I could feel my ancestors smiling on me in approval.

ELISE: Kaleo, since our first date twenty-six years ago to a Taiji/Qigong class, I've always been aware of how important this practice has been to your life's journey and your spiritual search – like it's an ancient stirring in you – in your blood.

KALEO: My ancestors were mostly Buddhists and Daoists. Somehow my father became Catholic and, as infants, my siblings and I were baptized Catholic. We went to parochial schools. After high school I served in the US Army in the late '60's, became more politically and socially aware, and totally rejected formal religion. Years later, you and I were practicing Taiji and Qigong, Yoga, Buddhist meditation, and prayers sacred to Hawaiian Lomilomi. I appreciate the foundations and values of my Christian upbringing, but in the Asian and Hawaiian practices I feel like I'm home.

ELISE: How has the practice of Taiji and Qigong influenced your creativity and your work in the world?

KALEO: I'm so grateful for the many teachers I've had. Forty years ago, while I studied for my art degrees in painting and lithography from the University of Hawai'i and the University of New Mexico, I also studied Taiji and Qigong. In California and Hawai'i I've also immersed myself in acupressure, Medical Qigong, Hawaiian Lomilomi massage, and hypnotherapy. The human body, the human soul, is like a canvas – there are textures, temperatures, shapes, colors, mysteries. For me, the visual arts and the healing modalities are all forms of creative prayer.

The creative and spiritual journey also encompasses one's work in the world. For you and me, it's in the forms of healing, teaching, writing, and art. I remember your concern about the inmates, and I know your work as a nurse in the San Francisco County Jails for twenty-five years was part of your spiritual path. I, too, loved teaching Qigong, meditation, and art-as-healing for about five years part-time in the same jail system. I remember how we'd be working in the same unit, and I'd be on the upper tier overlooking the lower tier, where you'd be nursing in the infirmary. The inmates and deputies thought it was pretty cute when we'd wave to each other.

For the past twenty-four years, we've also co-taught for many different venues, including John F. Kennedy's Arts and Consciousness program and Matthew Fox's University of Creation Spirituality. Our colleagues from different spiritual traditions, like Franciscan Sister Jose Hobday, Yoruba priestess Luisah Teish, Russill Paul with his gift of Yogic chanting, and so many others, really influenced us. Now, spiritually, I feel connected to Daoism and Buddhism, while you're also rooted in Catholicism, and we both integrate and honor all love-centered spiritual practices.

ELISE: Yes, we've led many students in Qigong, guided meditation and hypnotherapy, and art-as-healing processes. They're all about connecting with the soul and the Sacred within.

KALEO: Qigong is about loving-kindness, helping others, and gratitude in being part of the Divine mystery. I love how Qigong is a practice that infuses everyday life. We always remind our students that it's about being mindful, focused, and kind – kind to your body, to your soul, to others, and to God.

ELISE: We both know what a profound practice Qigong is. How would you describe its depths?

KALEO: It's Yin and Yang – meditation in movement, touching the inner depth and the outer expansiveness, integrating the light and the dark, reaching for Heaven and grounding in Earth.

It's a moving mantra. All the systems of the body – cardiovascular, musculoskeletal, cranial-sacral, lymphatic, respiratory, digestive, nervous, and meridian systems, even the conscious and subconscious minds – move in a synchronistic dance. Every cell breathes.

If you practice Qigong, in times of desperation, pain, and trials, it's always there to support and guide you. Especially when movement and meditation are combined, you change cellularly and neurologically, become healthier and happier, and have more gratitude in life. In the Microcosmic Orbit, with its powerful harmonizing influence on the chakras, you can feel Yin and Yang becoming more in balance – the dark and light, feminine and masculine, vulnerabilities and strengths, receiving and giving. The three Dan Tians of body, heart, and mind integrate. In the inner spaciousness and calm, you can hear the voice of deep inner wisdom. You find you make better decisions in life, as in choices of relationships and where you put your energy. You develop a trust in the Divine and feel you're invited to tap into its ocean of creativity, grace, wisdom, and loving-kindness.

I *know* that when my body dies, I return to this Divine ocean.

Qigong is also about being open to possibilities and to where and how the Qi wants to flow. When we met Reverend Steve Harms of Peace Lutheran Church, we connected with an open mind and a deeply spiritual and creative soul. The Abba-Imma Qigong is a child of that friendship.

QIGONG BASICS

Qigong (Chi Kung) is cultivation of Qi (Chi), your vital life's energy. It is an ancient practice rooted in Daosim and Chinese Medicine. It is related to Taiji, but Taiji is, at its foundation, a martial art with health benefits, while Qigong, in essence, is a healing art, which also strengthens and focuses one's inner warrior. Qigong facilitates the smooth and healthy flow of Qi through the organ-meridian system running through your body – rivers of energy flowing through your vital organs, your body's tissues, and near the surface of the skin where acu-points are located.

Qigong balances Yang and Yin, masculine and feminine, light and dark, and their long list of associated polarities. Yang and Yin are not separate but are interdependent. Whenever there is one extreme in Daoism, the other is close at hand. One can-not exist without the other.

Qigong helps to align the three energy fields, or Dan Tians, of the body, heart, and mind. It harvests energy from the abundant sources in the Heaven, Earth, and Environment for use by the body and releases waste Qi for recycling.

Practice Guidelines

- Choose a healthy environment, indoors or outdoors, to do Qigong.
- Dress comfortably. Wear flat, supportive shoes.
- Never look directly into the sun.
- Practice sitting or standing.
- Relax your body, mind, and breathing.
- Breathe fully and naturally. If you know it, engage Dan Tian breathing.
- Let your posture be aligned in a dynamic balance between strength and ease. If you know it, engage Zhan Zhuang sitting or standing meditation for proper alignment.
- If you experience discomfort, be kind to yourself, and modify the practice to suit your body. Do not go into pain, but stay in your comfort zone. If you are under care for health problems, consult with your provider prior to practicing Qigong.
- Practice Qigong as moving meditation. As your intention focuses on the present, feel past and future concerns fade.
- Try doing Qigong in different contexts – in the redwoods, by the ocean, indoors at your altar before your prayer/meditation time. Practice in your studio before creative process, and notice how your conscious and subconscious minds communicate with each other.

• Practice the Abba-Imma Qigong daily for one week and notice its positive effects on you. Practice it daily for three weeks and feel how you are transformed.

Practice with Kaleo and Elise and the Peace Lutheran congregation using the "Abba-Imma Chi Kung" video:
kaleoching.com/videos.html
or
peacejourney.org/adult-education-forums/

When you are comfortable with the form, practice on your own – just you, nature, and the Divine. As you feel inspired, share this embodied prayer with others.

Meditation and Journaling: Qi in Your Body
Close your eyes and look within. Do you notice any areas of tightness or contraction, of weakness or fatigue? Is your breathing constricted, your heart heavy? These indicate an imbalance of Qi. Do you notice any areas of ease? These indicate smooth Qi flow.

Now journal or draw what you felt and observed.

This is your body now. Notice how it changes after doing the Abba-Imma Qigong.

THE ABBA-IMMA QIGONG FORM

If you are doing Abba-Imma Qigong in nature during the day or evening, remember you are a child of Heaven and Earth. We come from the earth and the stars. Bask in the early morning sunlight or the evening starlight. Feel awe for the fact that it takes many years for starlight to reach you. Sense the temperature, texture, colors – the currents – of the light on your skin. Listen to the vibrations of the earth beneath you and of her environment around you. Breathe softly, gently, and let your body's inner vibrations sync to the outer vibrations. Feel awe for the power, intelligence, creativity, and mystery around you and within you.

Preparation: Abba-Imma Qigong can be done sitting or standing. Let the tip of your tongue rest on the upper palate of your mouth. Begin with your feet parallel and hips' distance apart. Feel the soles of your feet supported by Mother Earth. Feel the acu-point (Kidney 1) between the two balls on the sole of each foot open and pulsing. This is a portal to Earth Qi. Feel your energy roots sinking into the earth.

Let your arms rest at your sides. The center of each palm is open and relaxed. The heart of the palm (Pericardium 8 acu-point) is important for sensing, harvesting, and transmitting Qi.

Kidney 1

Pericardium 8

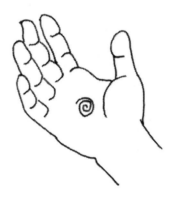

Wuji: Your body is aligned and relaxed. Your breathing is natural and flowing. Close your eyes, and let your attention journey inward – your mind savoring the stillness of the moment, your body receptive, your spirit open to the Divine. You have entered the state of Wuji.

Dan Tian: Focus your energy in the Dan Tian of your body, your storehouse of Qi, by bringing your hands to form a triangle facing your navel, and relish the mystery and power within.

Spread and raise your arms: Let your arms open and lift, floating like the wings of a bird toward Heaven. You are ready to speak your prayer.

Abba: Reach overhead to invoke the Father aspect of the Creator, the Yang. Feel gratitude as your palms touch and receive the shimmering light of the sun, moon, or stars and the numinous light of the Sacred.

Imma: Bring your hands in and down about eighteen inches in front of you to form a vessel to invoke the Mother aspect of the Creator, the Yin. Look at the ball of light in your palms. Understand that invoking both aspects, the Yin and Yang, of the Sacred beyond invites a balance of the Sacred within.

In heaven: Bring your hands together in prayer position about a foot in front of your heart. This draws the Abba-Imma energy down and into your heart to nourish love, compassion, and intimacy with self, others, and the Holy One.

Holy be your Name: With your palms in prayer position, close your eyes for a moment and savor the connection between the hearts of your palms and your heart center.

Your reign come: As you open and turn your palms into a downward facing triangle, feel your heart center open to ever-deepening relationship with the Divine.

Your yearning be done: Turn your hands to point your fingers, palms facing up, into your mid torso. Be aware of how you are a medium through which Divine yearning may be fulfilled on earth. The solar plexus, as the area of self-worth, is sometimes called the power center. Your personal power is most meaningful when in alignment with Divine yearning.

On earth: Pointing your hands toward Gaia, Mother Earth, invokes feminine, receptive Yin qualities. Kun, the natural force of Earth in Daoism/Qigong, is represented by a triple Yin trigram.

—— ——

—— ——

—— ——

Feel your feet grounding and your downward-pointing fingers siphoning nurturing Earth Qi. Relax your perineum at the center of the base of your torso, and feel Earth Qi rising up your legs and into your body.

As it is: Raising your arms in front of you to point to Heaven invokes masculine, assertive Yang qualities. Qian, the natural force of Heaven in Daoism/Qigong, is represented by a triple Yang trigram.

————————
————————
————————

Let the crown of your head, the area of an infant's soft and open fontanel, relax and receive the guidance of Heaven.

In heaven: Now turn your palms to face Heaven. As you open to the energy of Heaven, which is inspiring, uplifting, and energizing, you also open to the energy of Earth, which is grounding, centering, and calming.

Give us this day: As you bring your arms down, your hands form a basket about eighteen inches in front of your Dan Tian. In this basket feel the Heavenly nourishment you have harvested.

The bread we need: Now turn your hands to form a triangle in front of your Dan Tian, and press the Qi you have harvested into this storehouse. Feel the Qi flowing into your Dan Tian and throughout your abdomen, where your organs of digestion, elimination, and reproduction are located. Asking for just what you need ensures a balance – between having enough and leaving resources for others, between consuming and sharing. The open triangle is an acknowledgement of reliance on Divine and human endeavor to fulfill our creature needs.

Forgive us our wrongs: Turn your fingers to point inward, right fingers into your liver and gall bladder on your right side and left fingers into your spleen, pancreas, and stomach on your left side. The Liver/Gall Bladder organs and meridians in Chinese Medicine are associated with the Element Wood. An emotional challenge of Wood is anger, while emotional strengths of Wood are forgiveness, kindness, and purposeful growth. The Spleen-Pancreas/Stomach organs and meridians are associated with the Element Earth. An emotional challenge of Earth is worry, while emotional strengths of Earth are self-acceptance and trust.

As we forgive those who have wronged us: Now turn your fingers to point outward, palms up, in a gesture of openness. Feel your Pericardium 8 points, so powerful in channeling Qi, open and pulsing. This is a gesture of offering, of acceptance, of healing. Often Christ and Mother Mary are depicted with their hands outstretched in this gesture. The intention is a closing of the gap between self and others.

Guide us: Bring your arms up and out to your sides and draw your arms in, elbows and wrists flexing, fingers pointing outward.

Through life's trials: Then extend your arms, palms pressing outward to the right and left horizons. As your body forms the image of a cross, notice your heart's vulnerability, but also its strength, as an expression of your trust in and alignment with the Divine source.

And shelter us all from evil: Turn your palms, still outstretched, to face upward and receive Heavenly Qi. Above and beyond you is the vast expanse of the Cosmos. Feel yourself embraced by the ultimate protection, beyond words or imagination.

In your grace: Now raise your arms upward to point to Heaven, and feel Divine grace and inspiration flowing into your crown.

Your wisdom: Bring your palms together in prayer position as your hands descend to about twelve inches in front of your third eye, and feel Divine wisdom filling your mind.

And your love: Bring your hands, still in prayer position, down about twelve inches in front of your heart, and feel Divine love nourishing your soul.

Now: Bring your hands, forming an inward facing triangle, down about six inches in front of your navel, and feel Divine grace, wisdom, and love filling your body's Dan Tian, this vessel of Qi, profound creativity, and deep mystery.

And forever: Point your fingers inward and feel their Qi touching the Qi in your Dan Tian.

Amen: Now turn your fingers to point outward, palms up, and release your prayer into the world.

Store Qi: Store Qi in your Dan Tian, men right hand over left over navel, women left hand over right over navel. Feel the warmth and the fullness in your Dan Tian.

Journaling: Abba-Imma Qigong

Check in with yourself after doing this embodied Lord's Prayer. How does your body feel? How does your mind respond? What shifts do you notice in your soul?

What is your relationship like to God, Abba-Imma, Father-Mother?

How do you envision this practice supporting you as you move in the world?

THREE DAN TIANS

Dan Tian means "field of elixir." The three Dan Tians of mind, heart, and body are powerful centers of Qi, of energetic, physical, emotional, and spiritual intelligence.

The Dan Tian of the mind is where logic and imagination meet, where conscious thought and subconscious awareness dialogue.

The Dan Tian of the heart is where intimacy with self and others and wise protection meet, where compassion and the freedom to express and share your heart's truth support each other.

The main Dan Tian, of the body, in the center of your lower abdomen just below your navel, is where creative potential and the strength to manifest it meet, where your creative gifts and the gifts of the ancestors sustain each other. If the word "Dan Tian" is used alone, it refers to this Dan Tian.

Qigong integrates the three Dan Tians of mind, heart, and body. The Abba-Imma Qigong is praying with the mind, heart, and body.

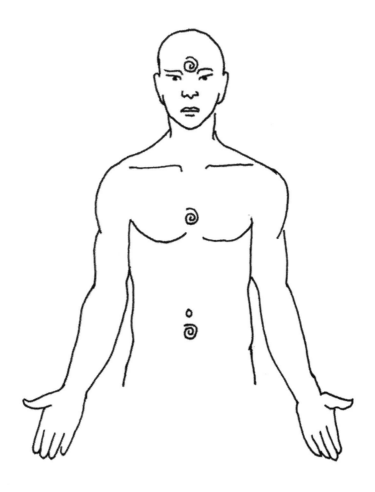

Three Dan Tians

Meditation and Journaling: Three Dan Tian Awareness

Center yourself in Wuji. Let your attention travel into the Dan Tian of your mind. What is the energy like there? Dense, light, electric? Notice any thought or sensation. Then let it go.

Now let your attention travel into the Dan Tian of your heart. What is the energy like there? Soft, excited, tranquil? Notice any emotion or sensation. Then let it go.

Now let your attention travel into the Dan Tian of your body. What is the energy like in your storehouse of Qi? Full, tingling, spiraling? Notice any gut awareness or sensation. Then let it go.

Now journal about your discoveries in each Dan Tian. How do your Dan Tians relate to each other? Do they feel integrated or disconnected? If you like, draw an outline of your body and depict your three Dan Tians. What colors, marks, and symbols show their energies?

Now do the Abba-Imma Qigong prayer. Then let yourself return to Wuji.

Meditation and Journaling: Three Dan Tian Blessing

Let your awareness travel up to a point in the Heavens far over your head. Welcome the gift of grace, wisdom, and love traveling from the zenith above you, down through the crown of your head, into the Dan Tian of your mind. Cherish this gift. Breathe. Let your mind bask in this blessing.

Now on an exhalation feel your breath descend from your mind into the Dan Tian of your heart. Feel your heart open to this gift. Breathe. Let your heart bathe in this blessing.

On an exhalation feel your breath sink from your heart into the Dan Tian of your body. Feel your lower Dan Tian receiving this gift. Feel your breath sinking deep into your core. Notice how it settles and spreads through this storehouse of Qi. Breathe and savor this blessing.

When you're ready, on an exhalation, feel your breath flow from your lower Dan Tian, through your legs and feet, and into the Earth. Gaia receives the blessing from Heaven through you, a vessel of Qi.

In your journal write/draw your experience of Divine grace, wisdom, and love permeating your three Dan Tians. If you like, draw an outline of your body. Within it, depict your three centers, of mind, heart, and body filled with this gift from the Heavens. Notice how each area has shifted in response.

QI BLESSING

After doing the Abba-Imma Qigong, you'll notice how calm and open your mind, heart, and body feel. There may be sensations like warmth, tingling, flowing Qi, or a soft cool wind blowing through you.

Doing the Abba-Imma Qigong with the Peace Lutheran congregation as part of the liturgy prepares us all for receiving the Body and Blood through the Eucharist. It can also be a preparation for sharing with others through the Qi Blessing.

Like a tree, you are constantly receiving nourishment from Heaven and Earth. In transmitting Qi, do not use your own limited Qi, but harvest from the abundant sources around you, including the Three Luminaries, the Sun, Moon, and Stars.

Find a time, day or night, to do this embodied Lord's Prayer in nature. Notice what luminous bodies are shining. Is the sun high and full overhead, or bouncing its light off the curves of clouds, or scattering its rays in warm pastels at dawn or dusk? Is the moon above you, low in the sky, or deep underfoot on the other side of the world? What is its phase – full golden glow, plump gibbous, slivered crescent? What stars do you recognize overhead at night? What stars are hiding behind the shimmer of day?

The cores of stars are like fiery wombs giving birth to the elements through nuclear fusion. When stars die, their elements disperse into the interstellar medium and become available for forming new stars and planets and for combining, under the right conditions, to form life. We are, indeed, made of stardust.

You have just completed the Abba-Imma Qigong. Feel how you are grounded in Earth, nourished by the healthy Environment around you, and filled with the vast Qi of Heaven. You are a child of the Cosmos!

Bring your hands to form a triangle in front of your navel, and feel your energy gathered in your Dan Tian. Now visualize someone with whom you would like to share a Qi Blessing. It may be someone whose creature needs are not being fulfilled, perhaps through loss of home or job or health; or someone whom you wish to forgive or to ask for forgiveness; or someone strained or broken by life's trials. Feel the energy of this person's presence before you.

Raise your arms out to your sides to point toward the distant horizons. Feel your arms gathering Qi.

Raise your arms overhead so your fingers stretch toward Heaven. Feel them gathering the radiant Qi of the sun, moon, or stars. Feel them gathering the grace, wisdom, and love of the Divine.

Bringing your arms down in front of you, shower the person's presence before you with this luminous Qi, as your arms descend to mind level.

Continue to bathe the presence before you with Qi as your arms descend to heart level.

Shower the presence before you with Qi as your arms descend to the level of the lower Dan Tian. Then release to Earth.

Do this Qi Blessing three times. Then release the energetic presence of this person. You may also want to bless yourself this way once. Then store Qi in your Dan Tian.

Journaling: Qi Blessing

Who was the person to whom you offered the Qi Blessing? What was the energy like of that person's presence before you? As you brought the light of sun, moon, or stars between your palms, what were its color and texture? As you welcomed the Creator's gift of grace, wisdom, and love, what were its color and texture? How did the energy of the presence before you change as a result of the Qi Blessing? How did your energy change? What happened to your thoughts and emotions from sharing this blessing?

ABBA-IMMA PRAYER

Abba, Imma, in heaven,
Holy be your Name.
Your reign come,
Your yearning be done,
On earth as it is in heaven.
Give us this day
The bread we need.
Forgive us our wrongs
As we forgive those who have wronged us.
Guide us through life's trials,
And shelter us all from evil,
In your grace, your wisdom, and your love,
Now and forever,
Amen.

Note: This page may be copied for sharing this prayer with others.

AUTHOR BIOS

STEVE HARMS, M Div (Masters of Divinity), MA Theatre Arts, is a Lutheran minister whose years in ministry have taken him from the streets of the Tenderloin in San Francisco to the streets of Danville, California, where he is Senior Pastor at Peace Lutheran Church. He has previously served as the President of the Interfaith Council of Contra Costa County and remains actively engaged in deepening Interfaith connections within the community. Steve provides compassionate pastoral care and is a gifted preacher who enjoys creative worship. Theologically empowered within his own tradition, he feels free to explore, learn about, encourage, and celebrate other faith traditions. He has maintained a long-standing involvement in and passion for justice advocacy and is a teacher of Tai Chi Chuan. Steve and his wife, Bev, have three sons. www.peacejourney.org

KALEO CHING, MA Art, CAMT (Certified Acupressure Massage Therapist), CCHT (Certified Clinical Hypnotherapist), MQG (Certified Medical Qigong practitioner), is an exhibiting artist and has a massage/acupressure/hypnotherapy practice.

ELISE DIRLAM CHING, BSN, MA Transpersonal Psychology, MA English, CAMT, CCHT, is an award-winning poet and worked as an RN at the San Francisco County Jail for twenty-five years.

For twenty-five years Kaleo and Elise have co-taught classes in Qigong, guided meditation, and transformative art at John F.

Kennedy University and other institutions in the San Francisco Bay Area, nationally, and internationally. www.kaleoching.com

Elise and Kaleo have coauthored five other books, including:
- *The Creative Art of Living, Dying, and Renewal: Your Journey through Stories, Qigong Meditation, Journaling, and Art* (© 2014, North Atlantic Books)
- *Chi and Creativity: Vital Energy and Your Inner Artist* (© 2007, Blue Snake Books)

If you'd like us to teach the Abba-Imma Qigong at your church or institution, contact lotus@kaleoching.com or steve@peacejourney.org

Made in the USA
San Bernardino, CA
04 March 2017